NATIONAL
GEOGRAPHIC

Ladders

NATIVE AMERICANS OF THE
SOUTHWEST

T0288413

The Mystery of the Ancient Pueblo

by Sheri Reda

It was a fall day in 1888. Two cowboys stumbled upon what looked like a tall city carved into a cliff. It looked empty and lonely. The only sounds were the whistling wind and the crunch of ice underfoot. Where were they?

The men had discovered the cliff dwellings, or homes, of the ancient Pueblo at Mesa Verde. Soon, **archaeologists** rushed there to learn more about these people of long ago.

The ancient Pueblo began living in the Four Corners region around A.D. 550. This is where Arizona, New Mexico, Colorado, and Utah meet. At first, the people lived atop **mesas**, or steep hills with flat tops. They hunted and gathered. They made beautiful baskets.

Later, the ancient Pueblo mostly moved off the mesas. They settled in villages and grew corn, beans, and squash. They lived in pithouses. A pithouse is a room built halfway underground with a roof. Still later, they made homes using **adobe**. Adobe is a mix of clay and straw that is formed into bricks.

Around 1200, the ancient Pueblo started living in cliff dwellings. Archaeologists think that perhaps they moved to these high places to be safe from enemies. Then, only a hundred years later, the ancient Pueblo left their cliff dwellings. No one knows why.

Descendants of the ancient Pueblo still live in the American Southwest. Among them are the Hopi and Zuni people. Even they aren't sure why their ancestors left the Four Corners area.

∧ This is Cliff Palace, the largest cliff dwelling at Mesa Verde. Mesa Verde is one of the best-preserved sites of the ancient Pueblo.

∨ Some of these petroglyphs depict legends, or traditional stories that may or may not be historically true. This one shows Kokopelli. He is a popular mythical figure in Southwest culture.

The ancient Pueblo used handprints like these in their rock art.

Messages from Long Ago

We can study ancient people by looking at the ruins of their homes and the pictures they drew.

The art of the ancient Pueblo explains their beliefs, struggles, and daily lives. Some of their art shows people hunting animals. Other art, like the picture at left, might tell about a legend or make a prediction about the future. But we don't know for sure. Just like the ancient Pueblo themselves, this artwork remains a mystery to us.

The ancient Pueblo made art using the materials they had. They made colored paints using nearby plants. They painted handprints on rock. They also used sharp stones to create **petroglyphs**, or rock carvings. The best rocks to carve petroglyphs on were dark on the outside. They had lighter stone underneath. As the stone was carved, the lighter rock showed through.

Rock art may last for years and years if left alone. However, humans can easily damage it. People visiting these rock art sites should be careful not to harm the art. The artwork of the ancient Pueblo still holds many secrets. Archaeologists and modern Pueblo are working together to understand the art's meaning.

Household Pottery

Pottery also provides clues about the lives of the ancient Pueblo. The people who lived in the cliff dwellings left behind pots and dishes. They also made clay figures. These ancient pieces are in amazingly good shape, considering their age. They look like they were made not long ago.

What's so great about old dishes and pots? They tell us about the everyday lives of the people who used them. Some pots have designs made by tribes living in other places. The foreign designs tell us the ancient Pueblo traded goods with other people.

Archaeologists also study the ways that household items were made. We know that the ancient Pueblo lived near mud that could be used to make clay, for example. Their clay pots and bowls prove that.

Broken pieces of old pottery are in the ancient Pueblo ruins. They give clues about the people who lived there. Different colors and patterns come from different time periods. These clues help us understand when the pottery was made.

Ancient Pueblo artists made this pottery figure sometime between A.D. 900 and 1200.

6

Most pottery was used for everyday activities, such as cooking or carrying water. Special pieces were used during ceremonies.

Empty Houses

So why did the ancient Pueblo leave their cliff dwellings? We know they left the Four Corners in about 1300. That was only about 100 years after they arrived. They moved south into Arizona, New Mexico, and Mexico. Many of their descendants still live in those places. This includes the Hopi and Zuni people.

Archaeologists have ideas about why the ancient Pueblo left. One idea is that drought, or a period of no rain, made it impossible for them to grow food. Another idea suggests that war upset their way of life. Or perhaps the groups living together couldn't get along and went their separate ways.

Some of the modern Pueblo, such as the Hopi and the Zuni, still live in adobe houses. Others live on top of mesas. Still others live in modern houses. They work with scientists and the government to protect the remains of ancient Pueblo civilization. They want people to learn about their culture. In time, they may also find out why the ancient Pueblo left their cliff dwellings behind.

∧ Some elements of ancient Pueblo culture live on in the dance, language, and art of modern Pueblo (shown here). They use bright colors and graphic patterns in their art and clothing.

∨ This deserted landscape in Utah was once home to a community of ancient Pueblo. Below is a group of stones that formed the round base of a kiva. A kiva is a building used for gatherings and ceremonies.

Check In What do pottery artifacts tell us about the lives of the ancient Pueblo?

Read to find out how a group of Navajo speakers helped the United States during World War II.

Rise of the Navajo Code Talkers

by Sheri Reda

illustrated by Owen Brozman

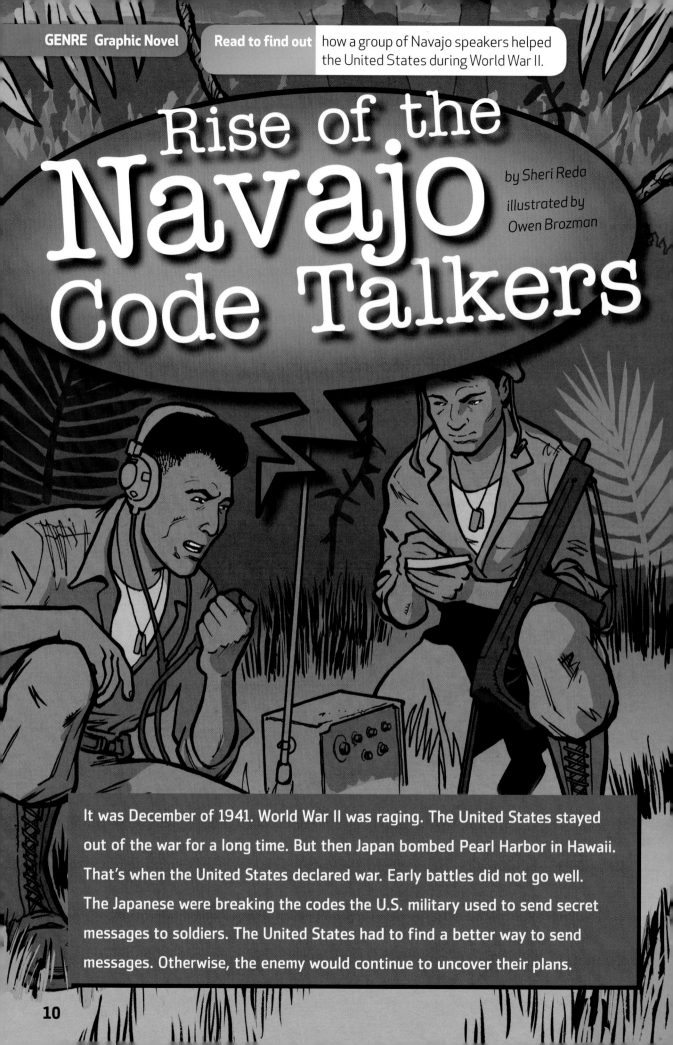

It was December of 1941. World War II was raging. The United States stayed out of the war for a long time. But then Japan bombed Pearl Harbor in Hawaii. That's when the United States declared war. Early battles did not go well. The Japanese were breaking the codes the U.S. military used to send secret messages to soldiers. The United States had to find a better way to send messages. Otherwise, the enemy would continue to uncover their plans.

A MAN NAMED PHILIP JOHNSTON HAD AN IDEA. HE SUSPECTED THAT A RARE SKILL FROM HIS PAST MIGHT BE THE SOLUTION. HE BROUGHT HIS IDEA TO AN ARMY MAJOR TO SEE IF IT MIGHT WORK.

MAJOR, I CAN GIVE YOU A CODE THAT WILL ALLOW YOU TO SEND AND RECEIVE MESSAGES ON A BATTLEFIELD SAFELY AND SECRETLY.

I THOUGHT NAVAJO WAS ONLY A SPOKEN LANGUAGE. HOW WOULD WE WRITE IT OUT?

WE COULD USE NAVAJO, SIR. IT'S A COMPLETE LANGUAGE, BUT ONLY ABOUT 28 NON-NAVAJOS IN THE WORLD KNOW IT.

WE WOULDN'T WRITE IT, SIR. THERE WOULD BE NO ANSWER KEYS AND NO WRITTEN CLUES. THE ENEMY WOULD HAVE NO WAY TO FIGURE IT OUT!

ALTHOUGH NOT A NATIVE AMERICAN HIMSELF, PHILIP HAD LEARNED NAVAJO AS A CHILD. HE HAD LIVED ON A NAVAJO RESERVATION WHERE HIS FATHER WORKED.

COUNT ME IN!

MEN, WE NEED YOU. THE NAVAJO HAVE A PROUD TRADITION AS WARRIORS. YOU CAN BE WARRIORS AGAIN, USING YOUR NAVAJO LANGUAGE AS A NEW CODE.

I VOLUNTEER!

THE NAVAJO HAVE ALWAYS BEEN GREAT WARRIORS. NOW WE HAVE A CHANCE TO SHOW IT!

JOHNSTON **RECRUITED**, OR INVITED, NAVAJO **CIVILIANS** TO JOIN THE WAR EFFORT. THE NAVAJO PEOPLE LIVED MOSTLY ON RESERVATIONS. THESE ARE LANDS ON WHICH NATIVE AMERICANS WERE FORCED TO LIVE BY THE U.S. GOVERNMENT. LIVING ON RESERVATIONS WAS DIFFICULT AT TIMES. BUT THE NAVAJO WERE A PROUD PEOPLE. NAVAJO **RECRUITS** WERE EAGER TO SERVE THEIR COUNTRY IN WARTIME.

THERE WERE NO NAVAJO WORDS FOR WARPLANES AND SHIPS. SO NAVAJO SOLDIERS INVENTED TERMS FOR THEM. THE NAVAJO RECRUITS LEARNED MORE THAN 200 WORDS AND PHRASES FOR THE CODE.

GREAT IDEA! IN NAVAJO, "CHICKEN HAWK" IS "GINI." THAT'LL BE THE CODE WORD FOR "DIVE BOMBER."

WE NEED A NAVAJO WORD FOR "DIVE BOMBER." HOW ABOUT "CHICKEN HAWK"?

THEY KEPT TRACK OF ALL THE NEW TERMS THEY'D INVENTED.

MILITARY CRAFT	NAVAJO WORD	MEANING OF NAVAJO WORD IN ENGLISH
Dive Bomber	Gini	Chicken Hawk
Torpedo Plane	Tas-chizzie	Swallow
Observation Plane	Ne-ahs-jah	Owl
Fighter Plane	Da-he-tih-hi	Hummingbird
Bomber Plane	Jav-sho	Buzzard
Transport Plane	Astah	Eagle
Battleship	Lo-tso	Whale
Aircraft Carrier	Tsidi-ney-ye-hi	Bird carrier
Submarine	Besh-lo	Iron fish

English Letter	English Word	Navajo Word
A	ANT	WOL-LA-CHEE
A	APPLE	BE-LA-SANA
A	AXE	TSE-NILL
B	BADGER	NA-HASH-CHID
B	BEAR	SHUSH
B	BARREL	TOISH-JEH
C	CAT	MOASI
C	COAL	TLA-GIN
C	COW	BA-GOSHI
D	DEER	BE
D	DEVIL	CHINDI
D	DOG	LHA-CHA-EH
E	EAR	AH-JAH
E	ELK	DZEH
E	EYE	AH-NAH

THEY NEEDED TO USE WORDS NOT ON THEIR LIST OF PLANES AND SHIPS. SO THEY SPELLED OUT THOSE WORDS IN CODE. THEY USED NAVAJO WORDS FOR LETTERS IN THE ENGLISH ALPHABET. LOOK AT THE CODE CHART ABOVE. WHAT ARE TWO WAYS OF SPELLING THE WORD "BEE"?

CODE TALKERS BECAME VERY SPECIAL MEMBERS OF THE SERVICE. THEY WERE EACH GIVEN TWO BODYGUARDS. THE BODYGUARDS PROTECTED THEM FROM ENEMY FIRE AND FROM PEOPLE WHO THOUGHT THEY WERE THE ENEMY!

AMERICA HONORS [THE] NATIVE AMERICANS WHO . . . GAVE THEIR COUNTRY A SERVICE ONLY THEY COULD GIVE. IN WAR, USING THEIR NATIVE LANGUAGE, THEY RELAYED SECRET MESSAGES THAT TURNED THE COURSE OF BATTLE . . . TODAY, WE GIVE THESE EXCEPTIONAL MARINES THE RECOGNITION THEY EARNED LONG AGO.

THEN, IN 2001, PRESIDENT GEORGE W. BUSH PRESENTED SPECIAL GOLD MEDALS TO THE FOUR ORIGINAL CODE TALKERS WHO WERE STILL LIVING. HE PRESENTED SILVER MEDALS TO THE DOZENS OF LIVING CODE TALKERS WHO CAME AFTER THIS GROUP.

MANY OF THE CODE TALKERS DID NOT LIVE LONG ENOUGH TO RECEIVE THESE HONORS.

CHESTER NEZ WAS THE LAST LIVING MEMBER OF THE ORIGINAL NAVAJO CODE TALKERS. HE GAVE A SPEECH IN 2013. NEZ TOLD ABOUT HIS EXPERIENCES IN THE WAR. HE SAID THAT THERE HAD TO BE A CODE TALKER ON DUTY AT ALL TIMES IN CASE A MESSAGE CAME THROUGH.

TOGETHER, THE ORIGINAL CODE TALKERS CREATED THE ONLY MILITARY CODE THAT REMAINED UNBROKEN IN WARTIME.

Check In How did the Navajo Code Talkers make a contribution to the war effort and serve their country?

ANIMAL SYMBOLISM
in the Southwest

by Brett Gover

HOPI WOVEN PLAQUE BASKET

> ## Turtle
> In many southwestern Native American cultures, the turtle is a symbol of Earth. They both move slowly and steadily. Can you find the turtle on this woven basket?

Animals play a big part in the culture, religion, and **mythology** of Native Americans of the Southwest. Many stories tell about animals that act like humans. They can speak and get angry. They can learn from mistakes, too. Sometimes the animals even have **divine** talents, such as changing the weather. But the stories also show an animal's strengths or weaknesses. They teach lessons about life.

Native Americans had great respect for animals. They put animal **symbols** in pottery designs and other art. These symbols do not just stand for the animal itself. They also stand for qualities the animal is thought to have.

ZUNI TERRA-COTTA OWL

⋀ Owl

Owls can see in the dark. They can spot tiny animals at a great distance. The owl represents wisdom, truth, and the ability to see things that others cannot. They are protectors of the home.

⋁ Frog

Frogs represent water, rain, and fertility. Frogs live both in water (when they are tadpoles) and on land. When tadpoles and frogs appear together in Native American artwork, they represent the cycle of life.

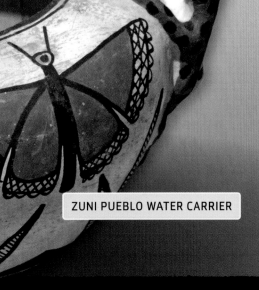

ZUNI PUEBLO WATER CARRIER

The Protector

If you met a bear, you'd be afraid. After all, they are large, fierce animals. To the Zuni people of New Mexico, however, the bear is a symbol of protection. They thought that if you put tasty food in front of a bear carving, the bear would guard your home.

The bear carving is called a fetish. A fetish is a small object that people believe has special powers or symbolic meaning. The Zuni create fetishes of animals that are important to them. They believe these animal fetishes have special healing powers. Fetishes often have straight or zigzagging arrows called heartlines. A heartline shows the path of the animal's breath. The Zuni believe that the heartline gives the fetish healing powers.

To the Zuni, bears stand for strength and the ability to change. The bear gives courage to face problems in life.

ZUNI BEAR FETISH

∧ The heartline carved into the side of this bear fetish shows the movement the animal's breath takes from its mouth toward its heart or soul.

⟩ The Zuni world was made up of six important directions. Each direction had its own color and guardian. The bear was the guardian of the west. The color for the west was blue, possibly for the blue of the ocean.

The Guardian

An eagle can soar in the sky and still hunt for prey far below. Its eyesight is amazing. Even from way up high, it can spot tiny animals on the ground. An eagle's eyes are nearly as large as human eyes. But it sees far more clearly than we do. Huge wings, powerful claws, and sharp eyesight make eagles fine hunters.

The southwestern Native Americans believe that the eagle guards the sky. The sky is one of their six sacred directions. The others are the four directions we know (north, south, east, west) and a direction underground. Way up high, the eagle carries people's prayers to the gods. The eagle symbolizes courage, wisdom, and strength.

ANCIENT EAGLE PENDANT

To the Zuni, the eagle is the guardian of the sky. The Zuni consider the eagle to be the younger brother of the wolf, who is guardian of the east.

This woven basket shows an image of an eagle. Many Native Americans use this kind of basket as a bowl.

HOPI WICKER BASKET

Have you ever wondered how the bald eagle got its name? After all, its head is not bald. The answer is that the word *bald* once meant "white."

The Healer

Lizards are common animals in the Southwest. Some are no bigger than your little finger. Others are as long as your arm. Many different kinds of lizards live in this region. It isn't surprising that southwestern Native Americans use lizard designs in their art.

The Gila monster is a big lizard, two feet long. This fork-tongued lizard spends most of its life underground in its burrow. It is one of only two lizards that have poison. The poison is harmful to humans. In spite of this, the Gila monster stands for long life in the mythology of southwestern Native Americans. In many legends, the Gila monster is the hero.

This lizard also symbolizes health, riches, protection, and happiness. Some people believe the Gila monster's skin can heal. Scientists have recently discovered that the lizard's poison may help fight some diseases.

Lizards decorate this basket. It was made long ago by the O'odham people in what is now south-central Arizona.

O'ODHAM BASKET

∨ Some lizards are brightly colored, while some are rather dull. The Gila monster's scales warn other animals to stay away.

Check In Describe some of the characteristics that these animals symbolize to the southwestern Native Americans.

How Coyote Stole the Sun

by Elizabeth Massie   illustrated by Richard Downs

Cultures all around the world tell folk tales. Many of these stories try to answer questions about nature. They may explain why grass is green, for example. This type of folk tale is called a *pourquoi* (poor-KWA) tale because pourquoi means "why" in French. The following Zuni story tells how winter came to be. It features Coyote, a popular trickster in many Native American stories.

Long ago, the land was dark. Though the weather was always warm, there was no light. Many animals struggled to live in the darkness, especially Coyote. He could not hunt for food because he could not see where he was going.

Coyote was jealous of Eagle, who could see in the dark. One day, Coyote called up to Eagle. The fierce bird sat perched on a boulder with a fat snake in her claws.

"I wish I could hunt as well as you," Coyote said. "But it is too dark and my eyes can't find my prey."

Eagle tipped her head, thinking, and then replied, "I know where there is light. I can take you there if you'd like."

"I'd like that," said Coyote. "Don't race too far ahead, or I'll lose sight of you."

After feeding the snake to her noisy children, Eagle flew west. Coyote ran after her. They traveled over flat stretches of desert, riverbeds, and hills.

Coyote stubbed his toe on a rock and shouted, "Ow! Slow down!"

"Why don't you watch where you're going?" called Eagle.

It was so dark Coyote couldn't see where he was going. But when he told Eagle this, Eagle sighed and kept on flying.

Finally, the two animals reached the outer parts of a village. In the center of the village, people were dancing and singing around a mysterious glowing box.

Coyote and Eagle watched from the shadows. Coyote blinked and squinted. He was not used to seeing light. He whispered to Eagle, "Let's steal the light and take it back with us!"

Eagle shook her feathery head and said, "That would be unfair. Let's ask to borrow it for a while."

Coyote snorted, rolled his eyes, and pointed to the dancers. "Just look at them. They enjoy the light far too much to let us borrow it. Please, Eagle, let's steal it. They've had it long enough, and now it's our turn!"

Eagle hesitated at first, but she finally agreed with Coyote. She swooped down and snatched the box of light with her claws. She flew away with Coyote racing along behind her.

As they hurried back toward the east, Coyote noticed how the light helped him see his way. He became very curious about the box of light. He wanted to peek inside. However, Eagle had the box in her claws, and he couldn't get near it.

"Eagle," he called, "let me carry the box for a while. Without the weight of that box, it will be much easier for you to fly."

Eagle replied, "No, thank you."

Coyote thought that Eagle might change her mind. Again he hollered, "Eagle, give me the box to carry, for then you can fly freely!"

Eagle replied politely, "No, thank you."

Much later, Coyote cried, "Please give me the box to carry, Eagle!"

Eagle at last agreed. She flew to the ground and handed the box to Coyote. Then she looked him in the eye and gave him a stern warning. "Do not open the box, for it is meant to stay shut. Just its glow is enough to let you see in the dark."

"I won't open it," promised Coyote. Actually, he was itching to see inside.

Eagle flew on ahead, leaving Coyote alone with the box of light.

For a while, Coyote carried the box across the desert. Finally, his curiosity got the best of him. He put the box down and looked at it carefully. He walked around it, touched it, and sniffed it. He even licked it to see if light tasted like anything. But none of this satisfied him.

"Enough," Coyote said to himself. "What harm can one quick look do?"

With that, Coyote nudged off the top of the box with his long nose.

Suddenly there was a loud *whoosh!* Coyote was knocked backward. The sun and moon flew out of the box and up into the sky.

As the bright sun flew higher into the sky, it got farther and farther away. The weather became cold and snowy. Coyote shivered and looked around. He hoped no other creature had seen what he had done.

But Eagle had seen Coyote. She flew back to where he sat covered in snow.

"I should never have given in to your begging," she said. "You have let out the sun. Now it is so far away that you've also brought cold weather to the world!"

Coyote hung his head in shame. Yes, he had brought light to the world. But he had also created winter.

Check In Describe the characters of Coyote and Eagle. How did their personalities affect their actions in the story?

Discuss

1. What connects the four selections you read in this book? What makes you think that?

2. Based on the evidence presented in the first selection, what do you think happened to the ancient Pueblo people?

3. How did the U. S. military and the Navajo work together during World War II? What were some of the challenges of using Navajo as the basis for a code?

4. What life lessons can we learn from Coyote's actions in the folk tale?

5. Which aspect of southwestern Native American culture do you want to learn more about? Why?